LIFE PATTERNS

LIFE PATTERNS

Responding to life's questions, crises and challenges

Jerry Schöttelndreier

Translated by Jakob M. Cornelis

HAWTHORN PRESS

Translated from the Dutch Originally published in Dutch as Levenslijnen

© Vrij Geestesleven, Zeist 1989

Typesetting by Bookman, Bristol.
Printed by Billings & Son Ltd, Worcester.
Cover by David Newbatt, design by Patrick Roe, Glevum Graphics.

Acknowledgements
Grateful acknowledgements for editorial assistance are made to Ruth Manson, by Jakob Cornelis

British Library Cataloguing in Publication Data

Schöttelndreier, Jerry
Life patterns: responding to life's questions, crisis & challenges.
1.Self-realisation
I.Title
158.1

ISBN 1 869890 272

'. . .Your majesty knows as well as I do that the future is pregnant with more eventualities than it can give birth to. And it is not impossible to hear some of them move in the womb of time. But only the situation of the moment decides which of these embryos is viable and will mature. . .'

Marguerite Yourcenar, *L'oeuvre au noir*.

Contents

Foreword

Working with the richness of material that our life story brings to each and everyone of us is a difficult task to take on. It is even more difficult and challenging to take on the task of conveying to people how this work can be done and the ways in which it can be helpful to the path of a human being's development. Jerry Schöttelndreier gave a series of lectures in which he attempted to introduce people to Biography work, that is the work with their own life story. In producing these lectures in book form we have all the advantages of the life of the original lectures and only a little disadvantage in that they were specifically given to a particular group.

Hitherto, there has been little guidance for people in how to work with their biographies. This book will help in three main ways: firstly, by giving a process by which any person can gain a greater understanding of his or herself; secondly, everybody is encouraged to take more responsibility for their own lives, and thirdly, the author emphasizes that the essence or the core of a person's life pattern helps each person to find their unique spirituality.

The book will be of special interest to people who are working professionally with other individuals' biographies and life questions. It will also be of great assistance to individuals who wish to get an overview of how to work with their own life story and how to seek out the patterns from the past which inevitably affect their activities and decisions in the present. The book clearly defines the differences in working with the past, the present, and the future, *and* in the dynamic balance in working between these three dimensions in a person's life.

There is much more emphasis on working with the past which the author indicates quite clearly is necessary in order that we can separate ourselves as objectively as possible from the past, and observe ourselves in the future, and help ourselves to make the decision for the future with an objective judgment of the past. In his conversational style he asks lots of questions and leaves the reader to answer them for her or himself. He explores the questions of old karma and new karma, and gives some insights into the deepening of fantasies or wishes into real life intentions.

When listening to a speaker give a lecture, it is always important to listen actively, and apply whatever the speaker is saying to your own particular situation and environment. Readers should remember this when reading this little book, so that they take examples and questions and apply them to their own particular life situation. Where the examples are given by men, then women should be encouraged to think of their own particular examples that would relate to themselves as a woman. Where the quotes are of a woman, then similarly, as a man reading the text, apply it to your life situation. With so little already in print about Biography work it is important to just recognise the significance of having such a direct introduction to working with your own Biography or the Biographies of other people.

So as you read, open your hearts, and your feelings, and your will to the development potential of the process which the author describes.

Jenny Daisley

Preface

Everyone knows those times in life when difficult choices have to be made. How conscious these choices are depends on many factors. There may be a tendency to drag obstacles that were not overcome in the past into the future. Or there may be an attempt, instead, to throw the entire past overboard as something that is finished. One's relation to the past often determines in part one's decisions for the future. Insight into one's own life, one's own biography and personality as well as recognizing the things that have something to do with oneself, and those that do not, can be vital factors in making decisions for the future. These may be decisions having to do with one's personal circumstances, such as relationships, where to live, family planning, or how to spend one's leisure time, or they may pertain to challenges at work.

This book is a practical guide for those who, individually or in a group, want to start looking for the patterns in their lives and the meaning of their existence. Even if one is faced with quite fundamental questions about one's life, one can arrive at some answers pertinent to one's own individuality and biography by means of the investigative process described here.

Jerry Schöttelndreier is a social practitioner and organization consultant. He works out of anthroposophy, and is associated with the NPI Institute for Organization Development in the Netherlands, founded by Dr. Bernard Lievegoed. He regularly facilitates biography workshops and offers individual biography counselling.

This book is based on two lectures given by Jerry Schöttelndreier, one on March 14, 1988, and the other on November 25, 1988, both in the Netherlands. In preparing the text, the directness of the spoken word has been preserved.

Introduction

In the past few years, it has become increasingly apparent that there is a growing and ever more serious interest in studying one's own life and contemplating one's own life situation. When you see what is available in bookstores, or what kind of courses are being offered, or when you regularly watch television, or read the newspaper every day, you notice that everywhere people are busy with and trying to do something about their own life situations. Of course, you wonder whether this is not just another fad; there have been plenty of them lately – everybody gets in on it, and the next thing you know, it has all been forgotten again. But I doubt this is the case. Perhaps you might say: Well, after all, there are many people at present who have plenty of leisure time – by choice or otherwise, whether because of early retirement, illness or unemployment – so that they simply have lots of time to pay attention to the study of their own biography. From my observation, however, contemplation is not exactly the kind of inner attitude being promoted these days, in spite of the abundance of leisure time.

As far as I am concerned, the interest people have in their own lives, and the importance they attribute to this, does not have the character of a mania or a fad. This interest, rather, shows a new step, a new movement in human development. It has a more definite, more meaningful significance than only something that will blow over again. I think it has something to do with an increasing awareness people have, which we can all observe if we pay attention – an increasing awareness of selfhood, of individuality.

I notice this all around me, particularly with young people. Take my own children, for instance; they asked questions at age sixteen or eighteen that simply never occurred to me at that age. And I encounter this in the organizations where I work as a consultant. Questions are raised there that have to do with a growing sense of self. In the courses I give, as well, people between the ages of twenty five and fifty five come together and, to a large extent, struggle with questions such as 'Who am I, really? What am I to do with my life? What do people think of me? What am I doing?' Very pertinent questions, indeed, although they are not always asked quite so explicitly, but when I spend two weeks or so with such people, it becomes quite clear what they actually came for.

This movement, this development, this process of increasing consciousness of self and awakening to our selfhood fits perfectly into the movement that started centuries ago, in which we all participate. It is a movement in which at first consciousness of self was asleep, in which man was part of a greater totality, subject to divine powers; then, in the Roman era, around the birth of Christ, an awakening to other people took place; and eventually there came to be increasing clarity with respect to what we are about as individuals, a concern with and insight into the lives we lead. It is a movement that in the future will perhaps lead to an ever greater sense of responsibility for one's own life.

I will not elaborate any further on this human development process from the point of view of increasing individuation. There is plenty of material on this subject in the literature. What I want to point out is that the interest in one's own life, and the course one's life takes – the interest in one's biography – is much more significant than it would be if it were only a fad. It is interesting to note that also from the medical profession there is an increasing interest in biographical counselling; dealing with someone's biography therapeutically and tying into it in the healing process is receiving more and more attention. This is good news!

I already mentioned the sort of questions I encounter in my work as a social practitioner and organization consultant when I facilitate large or small groups of people in biography studies. I talk to women and men who have questions such as 'Why did I actually become a doctor? I always wanted to become a pilot, but I never did!' Or 'Why am I unemployed?' (Of course I can answer 'Because you are one among hundreds of thousands,' but that is foolishness.) What matters to the questioner is why it is *he* or *she* who is unemployed, and what meaning this has in the context of his or her biography. I also get questions such as 'What should my objective be in the next twenty years? I am in a transitional phase. I want to start something new, but what? What should I devote the next period in my life to?'

Of course, in these sort of workshops, questions also come to the fore concerning home life. There are questions regarding youngsters, or relationships. 'Why has my third relationship gone on the rocks like the others?' Or, as someone wondered 'Why did I move twenty eight times?' People suddenly become aware of the question 'Why do I encounter so many similar situations in my life?' Isn't it interesting how people become aware of this? It really means one has already taken the first steps in the investigation of one's own life.

This brings me to questions of a more general nature that I recently saw formulated as follows 'Why do I have to live *this* life, and not another?' And 'Couldn't someone else live my life?' My colleague Alexander Bos refers to this in one of his books 'There is a fascinating Russian fairy-tale about a man who is not satisfied with his destiny. As an exception he is allowed to trade in his cross. The cross, with its vertical and horizontal members, is an image of the weft of life: the physical sheath the 'I' uses as an instrument on earth, and the occurrences that come to it from the outside. The man hands in his cross at the heavenly gate, and is then permitted to pick another at his leisure. In the heavenly warehouse they are staked high in endless variety, ready to be distributed to the souls descending to earth. After a long search the man finds a cross he thinks suits him perfectly. Peter gives it to him. It is his old cross. . .'

This image as cited by Alexander Bos is meaningful especially to those that ask themselves the questions mentioned above. For asking questions about, and of, one's own life, becoming aware of urgent questions about oneself, indicates a search for guidelines for that life: one wants to do something about one's own life. All of these questions point to a growing individual consciousness, to a greater consciousness of self. And this greater sense of self is what we need in order to find answers.

In order to arrive at answers, we have to make an attempt, to begin with, to create some distance between ourself and our own life. We have to try to look at it from a distance, and eventually to get a sense of responsibility for our own biography, although this occurs only at a more advanced stage. First we have to try to come to an understanding of small segments of our biography. And for this we have to overcome the feeling we all know, particularly when we are in a pessimistic mood, of 'Why are they doing this to me?'

Thus we see three stages in the relation to our biography. First 'Here I am, there is nothing I can do'; next 'I am beginning to understand'; and then 'I am the master of my own biography.' When you have reached this last stage, you have already gone far. For humanity in general, it will still take several generations, if not centuries, before this will become commonplace. I think it is extremely important, however, that we realize that gradually, by way of insight, we can start to get a sense of responsibility for our lives 'For better or for worse, it is *my* life, and I make *my own* choices!' This represents the choice between taking your life in hand, and letting it happen to you.

In the following I want to try and show you the various areas of investigation in a biography study, which factual material you should pay attention to, and the kind of questions that can help you get a handle on the important events of your life. How do we acquire relevant facts, and how do we interpret and use them? I will also go into the question of inner attitude during such a biographical investigation, and, finally, I will say something about possible results. First and foremost my discussion will be intended as an encouragement to get involved in your own biography. From the preceding, you will have gathered, I think, that I believe this is very meaningful in this day and age.

Still, I want to give you a warning. Don't expect quick results. It is not like 'Let's give it a go some rainy afternoon, and everything will fall into place.' To the contrary, it is often a long, drawn-out job, and you enter into a process that is not always an easy one. When you really start working with it seriously, you may run into matters concerning yourself that are not always pleasant. You will encounter things of which you will have to say 'Yes, that's right, that is how I did it,' after which you reach conclusions that may be painful. And this applies not only to the past. When you start working with it intensively, you may also arrive at painful choices for the future.

A final warning. To someone who has serious life problems, instead of simply questions, I would have to say: Don't start tinkering with it on your own, or even with a few 'nice' people you know. Find a specialist of some kind, a professional, so you can work on these problems with expert help. Do not tinker around with it. My story is concerned with offering help to people faced with questions about their lives that are manageable, although perhaps difficult. Do not expect therapy.

When we start to take a look at our lives, we can distinguish three areas for investigation, namely:

1. The *life world* – life at home;
2. The *learning world* – school life, self-development;
3. The *working world* – life at work.

Often the life questions someone has at the beginning of a biography study appear to belong specifically to one of these areas. After a while, questions pertaining to other areas also arise. Eventually it will turn out that many questions in the different spheres are connected.

All of these questions can relate to the *past*, as well as the *present* and the *future*. The urge to ask questions, which exists here and now, has its origin in either unanswered questions about the past, or in challenges of the future that have started to announce themselves.

With respect to the past, what matters in the first place is the gaining of insight ('Why did this happen this way? What was the situation, really? What are the connections?'). We can acquire an understanding of the past, therefore.

In the case of questions about our present situation, we have to try to get a correct emotional relation to them. These can be questions, for instance, having to do with relationships, employment, or, indeed, unemployment.

Finally, the questions may have to do with the future. These are questions where we have to discover what it is that we want, what kind of initiative will fire our enthusiasm.

What we see here, therefore, is a time dimension. This involves – if I may express it this way – what may be the fruits of the past, and the possibility of new fields to work on in the future, where we can still develop and search further. In this time dimension, as it turns out, some people tend to ask questions about their past, while others are more future oriented. My approach is to start with the past, and work through the present towards the future. Yet, it turns out, for every question, including those about the future, we need something from the past. What is not so obvious is that with queries related to the past we can frequently get a glimpse concerning the future.

The 'model' depicted below, which is based on the idea of 'dynamic judgment' developed by Alexander Bos, can help to keep track of our biography study.

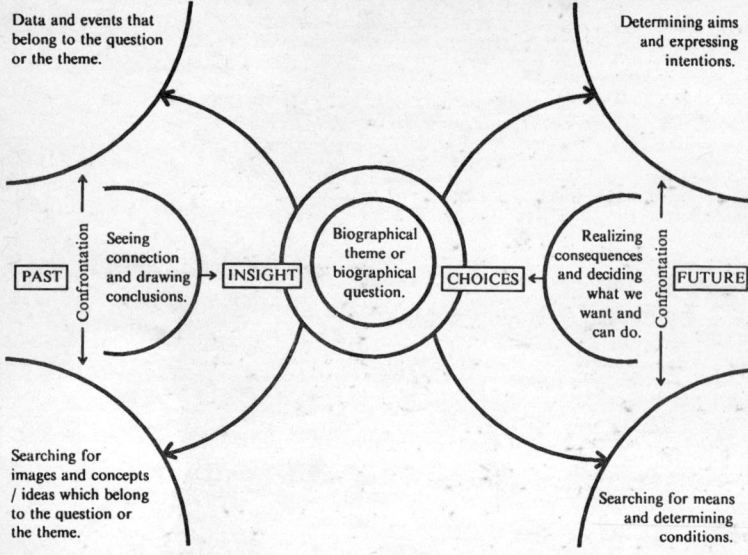

Data and events that belong to the question or the theme.

Determining aims and expressing intentions.

Confrontation

Seeing connection and drawing conclusions.

PAST → INSIGHT

Biographical theme or biographical question.

CHOICES

Realizing consequences and deciding what we want and can do.

Confrontation

FUTURE

Searching for images and concepts / ideas which belong to the question or the theme.

Searching for means and determining conditions.

Chapter One

Understanding the past

As I said, I will start by looking at the past. This is the part of our biography that is fixed. We can, so to speak, look it up in our diary. It can not be changed. It has happened, it is over and done with. This is why we can observe it quite accurately, and try to begin to understand it. We can try to approach the past with our thinking, and ask ourselves 'What happened? And what was the result?'

In this area I want to look at two aspects, which I call *inner* and *outer*. What I mean by 'inner' is what we carry with us when we come to earth, and what we do with this on earth, our inner biography. By 'outer' I mean all that which we seek out on earth as experiences, and encounters with other people, our outer biography. The inner world, therefore, derives from the past, and we carry it with us into the future. But the future is in part influenced by outer events. The inner aspect is, in fact, our 'spiritual impulse'.

PAST   PRESENT   FUTURE

Inner Biography

What did I bring with me ?
What was I given ?

What did I
(did I not) seek?
What did I
(did I not) meet?

What do I still have to do?
What will still happen to me?

Birth   Death

What did I (did I not)
do with it?
What happened (did
not happen) to it?

Outer Biography

Now

What we can say about our inner biography is that we brought it along when we were born. We could also say, however, that it was imposed on us, more or less as follows 'I can't help it. After all, it was part of my "baggage," which I found waiting at my birth.' This is one point of view. An entirely different attitude is the one where you say 'I selected it myself.' I will not elaborate any further on the background for these two points of view, but it is clear that there is a difference.

Similarly, we may ask 'What did I do with this baggage?' Or, if we take the other point of view 'What happened to this baggage?' You see the difference?

We can recognize the same active (proactive) and passive (reactive) viewpoints in questions such as, on the one hand 'What did I seek out on earth? What have I avoided?', and, on the other hand 'What did I run into, what did life bring to me?' Or, if for a moment we get ahead of my story 'What am I after?', compared with 'What will happen to me, what is in store for me?'

You probably realize that I take the viewpoint of the individual being actively involved, him or herself, consciously or unconsciously, in all of the events and encounters, in all of the possibilities and impossibilities, and in all of the opportunities we had or missed.

Where do we start when we want to gather facts about our past? In all three areas of study – the life world, the learning world, and the working world – I want to look at the *physical* and also the *non-physical* sides.

Let us start by looking at the inner aspect of what we had with us at birth in the physical realm. Do we have a male or a female body? There are distinct possibilities associated with each, but also impossibilities. Is it a healthy or a sickly body? Is it complete or incomplete? What happened to this body, subsequently? What kind of illnesses did we get – or, perhaps, find? Is it a robust or a delicate body? Attractive or unattractive? What kind of heritage is it that we brought along to earth, and what were the possibilities and the limitations inherent in this given factor, this body?

In the non-physical we are also dealing with certain given factors. How, for instance, have our temperament and our character affected our life? Temperament does not necessarily play only a negative role. It may have helped to make some things possible that would have been impossible otherwise. We may ask ourselves 'What about my dreamy tendencies? What were the consequences of those?' In short 'What kind of experiences have our character and temperament brought to us, in our youth as well as later on?'

Besides the inner area, we also have to examine our outer world. Which influences from outside have we sought out, have we encountered?

When we look at our home life first – our life world (for this is what we encountered first in our life) – we come to a vital question 'What kind of influence has this home life, this home environment, had on us?' Where did we grow up? Was it in the woods, or in an urban mass of stone? Where did we 'awaken'? Memories of this are a very important entry into a biography study. Did we spend our youth in a big city or a small village? In a large or a small house? On the fifteenth floor or at ground level? Where did we spend our first years? Abroad or at home?

Subsequently we can also examine the psychological environment of our childhood. Was it an artistic environment? Was it a cosy home, or a chill place, or was it crowded? What can help here is to concentrate on the people around us during our childhood. Take a look at the people that pass before your mind's eye when you close your eyes and recall the images of your childhood. Who do we see? Perhaps our parents, if we were so lucky, but perhaps also other people who took care of us. How was this in the further course of our biography? Which people did we encounter later? Was it busy around us or quiet? Were there other children, or were we alone? Was it so busy at home that we could never find a quiet spot of our own? Or did we have to go out in order to meet other children because there were no other children at home? What was the 'colour' of our home life? Were we the only boy, with a mother, a lot of sisters, and a lot of aunts, but no father? Or did we have a more male-dominated environment, i.e., was there a female or a male 'colour'? Were both our parents at home, or were they divorced or widowed. And what was our own position in the family? Were we the oldest, who always had to be the most sensible, or the youngest, who could get away with anything? Or were we the famous second? Did we have many uncles and aunts? Perhaps the grandparents were still alive, or, on the other hand, there may have been few relatives. What kind of atmosphere was there at home? What did the grown-ups talk about (assuming they talked at all)? Were these profound conversations, or more artistic in nature? Or was the talk practical, or technical, or having to do with business? Everyone can capture this kind of atmosphere for themselves.

We can also think of our upbringing. Could we do as we pleased, was it a free-for-all at home, or was it, instead, very strict? Did we have to go to our friends' houses to have fun because we were never allowed to do anything at home? Or was the house always so crowded that it was never very comfortable there? And what about our sense of security in this family? Was it a real home, or did we feel more at home at our friends' houses? Was it a kind of 'nest', or did we always have to be on our guard that something wouldn't go wrong?

This way, there arises a broad spectrum of impressions, from the physical environment to the spiritual aspects of our home life, i.e., the ideals that may have been discussed and/or pursued at home.

This is also the way to look at our learning world. There, too, we can explore the entire spectrum, from the physical, through the psychological, to the spiritual. We can collect straight facts, and take an inventory. We can start with questions such as 'What did our kindergarden look like? And our primary school? One of my own first impressions of school is of a fairly large room, with old-fashioned school benches with the seat and desk in one piece, with hooks at the side for hanging slates and sponges. One row was class one, the next row class two, and the third was class three. And there was one teacher up front. This was quite different, of course, from present school systems, with 2400 children and 240 teachers, plus a large administrative staff. Well, this is the sort of thing I had in mind – what kind of schools were we in, including the physical aspects?

Next we can look at our relationship to the people we encountered in these schools. Were we ourselves 'popular'? Did we like going to school? And what was the reason why we liked going to school? Of course, we went because Mum and Dad said we had to, but how did we feel about it ourselves? Did we go because all our friends were there, or was it because we liked the teacher? And when the contents of the lessons began to take on a greater significance for us and we developed preferences for certain subjects, was this because of the subjects themselves or was it rather because of our admiration for the teachers that taught them?

You can also say something about your relation to things. How did you relate to something? Was it mostly (and perhaps still is) a direct relation to the things themselves, or one via other people? What was the role other people played? How did you relate to authority, for example? With difficulty, or did you take authority for granted? And what about solidarity? Etc.

We can get further important information when we try and discover the relationship between home and school. Sometimes this can be taken for granted, but in many cases there may be differences in the way different families relate to the school. Did we live close to school, or did we have to travel quite a distance, so that it was always difficult to bring friends home? Was there any interest at home in what we learned at school and for the way in which we learned it, or couldn't they care less? What was the relation between our parents and the teachers at school? (I know of one case where a child's mother was also his teacher. So he could never get away from his teacher *or* his mother!) In this way everyone can learn different facts from their learning life.

Following the learning life, we come to the area of work – our work world. For many of us this is an extremely important area. In the past it was important mainly to men, but at present, fortunately, also more and more to women. How has this area contributed to our development? I assume that it has contributed something, at least, but this does not always have to be the case, which in itself is, of course, quite a problem. What applies to everyone, in every case, is the question 'What kinds of experience have we had in our working life?' And also 'How have changes in our work affected us? How did such changes come about? What kinds of transformation have we gone through?' What I frequently come across in the case of men of forty to forty five years of age who have been in a technical profession for twenty to twenty five years is that they say 'Yes, but now I've had enough. Now I want to deal with real problems, with people. It was OK. I've enjoyed engineering, but now other things are becoming important.' How did these people come to have such a change of mind? If we ourselves experienced such a transformation in our working life, how did it come about?

It is also worthwhile to look at the different locations where we have worked. How did we come to be in these places? Was this due to our own initiative, or were we moved there? Were we promoted regularly, or did we have to go after promotion ourselves? Or did promotion not matter to us at all?

How, we may also ask, did we relate to the firm we worked for? My father, for instance, was a 'member' of 'The Royal'. (Nowadays we would say he worked at Shell). What he did and where he was did not matter to him. He was (and in a way still is, in spite of the fact he is in his nineties and long since retired) a 'Royal' man. It was his whole life. When you see him, you have to say 'Of course, there goes a 'Royal'.' This, you see, is how this company deals with its people. It forms them, whether they are black, white or red. You can hear it and see it, at least when you have an eye for that sort of thing. For my father it was not important what he did. It was the business that was important. For others it is their profession that is important. For instance 'I am an accountant. No matter where I am in the whole wide world, no matter who I work for, I am an accountant first. That is what counts – that is my working world.' These are the sorts of questions we have to ask ourselves – what is our connection to our work? The people, the organization, or our profession or vocation? There can be a lot of different answers.

It is also important to find out how we relate to the product of the organization we work for. This is not a matter of what kind of organization it is (such as in 'The Royal'), but of what is produced there. How has this product affected us? I have spoken with people who worked in the diamond industry, the oil industry, utilities, or mining, and they all related in different ways to the product they contributed to.

What can also be important is to evaluate to what degree our working world was a secure one. Did we have a government job (this used to be considered quite 'safe'), or are we in a turbulent commercial enterprise where we can get the boot if we don't meet our quota.

And what is the style of the organization or firm we work for? Is it a style that fits our psyche, or do we not really feel at home in it? What kind of inner connection do we have with it?

If we have changed jobs often, we can examine the relation between the different functions we have had. Were they all more or less the same, or is there hardly a discernible common thread? Is it possible to detect some similarities in spite of the different titles we have carried? Is there, for instance, a commercial overtone, or a more technical one, or did we have a lot to do with personnel. In short, is there a 'string' for the different 'beads' to make a necklace?

This perspective is useful when our life questions have to do with what kind of work we should do in our next life period. The questions mentioned may be helpful in making a choice for the next twenty years. What can we discover about ourselves in the jobs we have had for the past twenty years? Or do we have the feeling these jobs reveal nothing about us. This seems almost impossible, but there are people who experience it in this way. This in itself can say much about one's life.

Once we have collected many data and facts (they may have been collected in many different ways – it does not have to be from memory only, but may include diaries, photographs, conversations with relatives and older friends, etc.) we can continue with the next step in our biography study. This is the step I already referred to, that of 'stringing beads'. We now have to ask how all this information is *related*. Can we discover any pattern, or perhaps several patterns?

There are a few questions that may assist us. The first is: *Which periods can I now distinguish in my life?* I do not mean the kind of periods described according to various views in developmental psychology, such as the seven-year periods of Lievegoed. These are periods that apply to all of us. No, what matters here is which shorter and longer periods are distinguishable in *my* life in particular. If we can discover these periods, we can name them. We may, for instance, have had an 'exploratory period', or an 'introvert period', followed by an 'explosive period'. These names are to be chosen in such a way that we can really feel 'Yes, that is how it was!'

A second question to help us may be: *Which life themes, motifs, become visible?* Which are the things that reappear again and again? It does not always have to appear in the same form, but there may be similarities. Perhaps a theme does not appear for a certain length of time, but then, suddenly, we see it emerge again. This is different, therefore, from the life periods. There it was a case of one period after another. A life theme, however, may not be visible for a time, and then suddenly re-emerge. The theme could be 'music'; or our relationship with other people; or problems, for instance, with 'authority'. (For example 'It used to be that I had a problem with my father; now I experience the same thing with my boss. I don't understand it – after all, I am not that hard to get along with! And yet I always come into conflict with authority.') When these life themes, these motifs, have been found, we can 'tag' them also; as a rule this will be easier than naming the different life periods.

Another question is: *Are there certain situations, experiences, or encounters that recur again and again?* When I look at my own life, I notice that on a number of occasions I got myself into difficult situations that resembled each other. I know that if I had thought about it beforehand I would never have entered into them. And yet these situations had real significance in the course of my life. What was it, then, that made me go for these situations? I always say: It was the (unconscious) will; my feet did it, or my hands, but not my head. What matters in this question, therefore, is that we develop an eye for these moments, which have co-determined our life, and are therefore truly part of us.

In general, what is also a useful approach to the collection of data, although less specific than the three preceding questions, is *underlining the truly important*. We have to get a feel for the truly important events in our life, for the milestones, the crisis points, for those moments of which we feel: that is where my life took a new turn, that is where it reached a turning point. We then come to see what far-reaching consequences the important decision or meeting had. This way we can get a picture of the real causes of new developments in our life. All kinds of connections between events that were not obvious before become visible when we work on this intensively. As a result, we may get a more coherent picture of our biography. Connections between the three areas (living, learning, and working) may be clarified.

Finally, I want to say something about our inner attitude while looking at our past, before I continue with the present. In order to make the work with the past productive, we have to try to create as much of a separation as we can between ourselves as we are now and as we were in the past, and to observe as objectively as possible. Although it will be quite difficult, it is nevertheless important *not to judge* according to our present criteria. Such a judgement is generally not helpful to clear and exact observation. For passing a judgement means looking at a situation in the past, our own life in this case, from the perspective of today. And this applies particularly, of course, to those events in our life of which we say 'If I could do it all over, I would do it quite differently.' But we did not do it differently, and perhaps this was quite justified at that time, for then we did not know what has happened since, even though we know it now. We can not change the past, so we have to take care to separate ourselves from it.

This is not so easy. We all know of events we have not come to terms with inwardly yet. In an investigation of the past, we inevitably run into such events, and the emotions associated with them, if we were not already aware of them. For instance, how you felt about having chosen the wrong subject in college, or about a problematic relationship, or an unsuccessful job application. These are the kinds of problems which, to play it safe, we may have pushed away, pushed aside, thinking 'That was embarrassing, forget it, let's not have anything to do with it anymore.' But when we start a biography study, these problems inevitably rear their ugly head, and then the thing is to say 'OK, let's deal with it once and for all', like Parsifal, the hero of the medieval story by that name – not avoiding the problems, but meeting them head-on.

In working through one's biography, one has to look at the problems clearly and objectively – as if one were someone else, as if one were looking at someone else's questions. Outwardly there is distance already: the distance of the years since the problem occurred. But we still need inner distance. What can be helpful here is if other people look with us. They already have the inner distance, for it was not their problem. This is the idea behind doing this kind of work together with others. For the more objectively we deal with our past, the more space and freedom we get for the future.

Suppose we took the norms and values we held in the past with us into the future. Suppose we did not disengage ourselves from the past at all. What would there be left to decide for the future? The norms would be fixed for the future as well. It is important, therefore, first to have 'cleaned house' with respect to the past, to have inwardly come to terms with it, to be reconciled with it. Only then can we say 'Yes, I did it in such and such a way, and the consequences were such and such. Whether I like it or not is no longer interesting. This is simply the result, and that is part of my record. So be it, that is how it was . . . and now let's get on with my life – now and towards the future.'

Chapter Two

Finding a relation to the present

What we have done so far, with respect to the past, is to collect as many facts as possible in order to determine whether we could find elements that provide us with some insight into our own life. Now we will see whether we can find a way to relate to the present, to our present life. We will do this at first by considering what has become of us since the past. (*What is the relation between present and past?*). Subsequently – and here our biography study takes a new turn – we will try to get a glimpse of the future. (*What is the relation between present and future?*).

Hopefully we have succeeded in gaining the necessary clarity and objectivity with respect to the past, and created an inner distance from it. Even if we have not always succeeded completely, we have still obtained a picture of the past that is as frank as we could make it. With this candid picture, we arrive in a different realm – the realm of the present. We are in the middle of it. We are surrounded by it. It is here now! What may be different for different people is that for some the present started a year **ago**, and for others it is starting from moment to moment. Everyone has to determine this for him/herself. What applies to everyone, however, is that, since we are in the middle of the present, since we are so close to it, we have an emotional relation to our life as it is now. This emotional relation is something we have to make use of.

As I have said, this emotional relation to the present can have different nuances. We may still have a strong relation to the past. ('What has come of all this in the present? What have I got out of it?'), but similarly we may experience being strongly drawn to the future ('What can I already see of the future? What has become visible in the other direction, what is already streaming into me?'). In both instances, these questions are so close at hand that we need our feelings in order to relate to them.

When we now look at the past, what matters is that we continue the lines we started drawing in our youth on into the present. Here, too, we can look at both our inner and our outer world. What has become of all those things of the past? What do they look like now?

I will start by looking at the inner aspect, at the *actor*, the player. How have the physical attributes, the bodily aspects, worked until now? What has happened to them? What have we done with them? And what have we *not* done? What had we expected of this physical instrument? What had we hoped for? Had it been our intention to win a gold medal at the Olympics with it? Or become a pilot? Is it clear that whatever has not been successful was not feasible to begin with?

What have we experienced from this bodily part of ourselves? How have we handled it? Have we used our body well, or not? Or have we even misused it, perhaps? And how did we feel about that deep down?

It is important that we ask these questions in a time perspective. So: How was it at first, and how is it now? Is there any evidence of a developmental trend? Has our relation to this physical aspect changed over time?

Then we come to the next level, the psychological level. How have we dealt with our temperament? And how has our temperament affected us? Are we still as sanguine as before? Or as phlegmatic? Do we still succumb to melancholic moods, or have we learned how to handle these? Do we still react in a choleric manner, i.e., are we still so irascible? What have we accomplished owing to our temperament, and what in spite of it?

And besides our temperament, we can also look at our character. A useful aid is the typology of Max Stibbe: the ego-conscious type, the dreamy type, the aggressor, the aesthetic type, the dominant type, the mobile type, and the radiant type. What type are we? And how have we developed with respect to this? Which of the seven qualities mentioned fits us best?

We can enter into our being still deeper, however, and try to discover how we relate to the signs of the zodiac – at least, if we have a connection to this point of view. We then enter the realm of *personality*, about which the biologist Frits Julius wrote two fascinating books: *The Twelve Drives* and *The Imagery of the Zodiac*.[1]

Finally, also on the psychological level, we can look at our *inner orientation*. Three categories are helpful here: the *time orientation* (i.e. is the polarity past-future dominant in our life?); the *human orientation* (i.e. do we have a predilection for the social aspect of life, including the male-female polarity, which plays an important role within ourselves and our relationship with others?); and the *world orientation* (i.e. is the emphasis in our life on our relation to the world – do we identify with the heaven-earth polarity?).

Following the psychological level, we can examine how we handled our heritage at the spiritual level. This raises questions such as: Do we recognize existential choices in our past, and, if so, how have we dealt with them? What do these choices show us? What do we begin to recognize as the central task in our life? What have we taken up in the way of causes, and have we made any sacrifices for them? Do we have a connection with a particular spiritual path? What kind of existential questions do we struggle with?

We can also ask ourselves what we have done with our *talents*, our abilities and our limitations. What have we utilized, developed? What has remained undeveloped?

I will also give a few guidelines as to how to look at the outer aspects – our 'stage'. As opposed to our inner being and its development, where our inward relation to things is what matters, we have to do now with that which we actually encounter in our life, that which we seek out. Emotionally, for instance, we can have a human orientation, while in practice we encounter few opportunities to develop in this respect, whatever the reason may be (and perhaps this is what is actually important in our biographic research).

When we take a look at our present life situation or work situation, what do we see there? What does it look like? I will just mention a few examples, for this can, of course, become an extensive search, depending on the life questions we have. For example, we may be looking for our connection to what I call the *upper world*, the world

---

1   For those readers who have no connection to the temperament, planetary and zodiac psychosophies, informed by anthroposophy, or have no access to information regarding these subjects, other psychological typologies will serve the same purpose, i.e., how was I then, how am I now. (The author)

of the arts, religion and science. Is that our world? Or are we, in fact, always concerned with other people – at home or at work? Is the *social world* our world, really? Whatever form it takes, caring, or serving, or leading, is our life determined mainly by the intercourse we have with other people? Or is the *earthly world*, the material world, our environment? This can be our garden, our home, or our car –we are always busy with it. But it can also be something like the following, which is what a physiotherapist was concerned with, who said 'The human body – that is what I relate to, that is my task.'

If our interest lies in the social world, an interesting diagnostic aid is to make a *sociogram*. We take a large sheet of paper, and draw ourselves in the centre. Around this we draw a number of concentric circles, and on these we write the names of people we have met in the past few months, or in the past few years. With the aid of our diary, we can perhaps obtain a reasonably complete list of people with whom we have been in contact. What we do is, we place the people with whom we keep in close contact, or with whom we feel a close connection, on a circle close to the centre, close to ourselves, therefore, and those with whom we have had a more sporadic or casual contact we place further away from the centre. In this way we obtain an interesting pattern, which we work out further with heavy and thin connecting lines between ourselves and the names on the circles around us. Finally, we turn these lines into arrows, in such a way that the arrow points inward in the case of contacts that came about as a result of our being approached or visited, and points outwards if we ourselves took the initiative for the meeting(s). Now, what does this pattern look like? Are we always the ones to make contact? Is it becoming clear that we always have to go visiting because otherwise we would never see a soul? Or do we always receive the visits? Do we have hardly a moment to ourselves because people always drop by because they want something from us? And what about the frequency of the meetings? Are there many heavy connecting lines, or do we see most people only sporadically. And are there many people close around us, or is there mostly a distance?

The sociogram makes it quite obvious, and sometimes painfully so, what our relation is to the people around us.

But besides the people around us, we can also look at the *situations* we encounter or seek out, or those we avoid. What is it like – this stage on which we are the actor? How does our environment affect us, and how do we affect the environment? Do we exploit our environment, or are we exploited by it? Do we, for instance, always impose our will on others, or is it a case of often having the feeling 'What about me?' This is a question mothers and housewives often ask themselves, and it is a good question, for looking at the stage is at least as important as looking at the actor on this stage. What are the dynamics on that stage?

In order to know ourselves, it is ourselves we have to look at, of course. But that is only part of the truth, for the stage we chose for our act contains something of ourselves as well. It is no coincidence that everybody is where he or she is. The fact that I give lectures and courses is, of course, something I myself have chosen to do, even though I do not find it easy at all to appear before a sizeable crowd. This is one of the decisions I made earlier on. Not with my head, for if I had made only a rational decision, I would have said 'But I don't want to do this at all, I am no good at it. I'd much rather sit in the audience listening to a speaker than being the speaker myself.' Nevertheless, here I am, the speaker.

This applies to all of us: the stage has as much to do with us as the actor. All of the things and people around us are 'mirrors', to the left and to the right, in front and behind, below and above – all that which we have gathered around us is part of ourselves. It has all come to us, and we have sought it out. So we must take a good look in these mirrors, in a way similar to that in which we look over a room when we visit someone for the first time. When the hostess or host has gone to the kitchen for a moment to make coffee, and we remain behind alone in the living room, we ask ourselves, 'Would I ever buy a lamp like that? Or a settee like this? And what kind of books are those in the book case? And, look at that painting!' And then, when the host or hostess returns, we suddenly sit straight again. For a moment we were able to peek 'inside', for someone's environment makes something visible about him/her. I am convinced that there is no coincidence in all the things we collect and exhibit around us, in the people around us – whom we go and visit. All this belongs to us, so we have to pay attention to it.

To complete this part of our biography study, concerning our present relation to the past, we have to ask ourselves a couple of extremely important questions, which I would simply call the *why* question and the *wherefore* question.

The why question can be asked in relation to some of the

momentous events in our life, or to certain themes, or in relation to the stage on which we find ourself. Why has this or that happened? Why do we always get into fights? Why do we always meet certain kinds of people? Why do we always get into these difficult situations? Why does this or that always happen to us? Why did we actually enter into this relationship? Why did we choose this or that kind of work? Why, for heaven's sake, did we quit? Why did we get the sack?

And then the wherefore question: What did we get out of it? It does not matter whether it was much fun (which, of course, it may be), but the question is, what was it all for? What was made possible by breaking off a relationship, what was the result? What did this initiate for us? What kind of space has been created following a certain moment or event? I once had someone in a course who was quite worried about the relationship he had with his mother. This had bothered him for years. Only when he dared ask himself 'What was it exactly that happened between us, and what were the consequences of this?', and subsequently 'But why?', was some space created in his soul. But first he had to 'stand beside himself ', talk about it with others, and look at it the same way as the others, from the outside, as a stranger. And gradually it became clear to him that it was not fruitful to hang on to the 'old' feelings, that it was better to inquire into what had actually happened, and what effect this had had. Fortunately, he had never before met any of the other people in the course. It seems most people find it easier to speak about intimate problems with strangers than with those who are close to them. In any case, in the end this man sorted it all out. He even said at the end of the course 'Maybe I'll write the "old lady" a letter', and this after having had no contact with her for years! This demonstrates how beneficial it is to honestly ask – if possible with other people's help, in a group – 'why' and 'wherefore' questions.

Chapter Three

The future announces itself

Now that we have charted the past and our present relation to it, we will look in another direction: towards the future. This is a completely different but equally interesting scene. With our eyes on the future, we will first have to see what this future is already telling us, so that we can add these indications to our balance sheet of the present. For this is what we are still doing, asking: What is our situation now? We are putting the debits and the credits on our balance sheet. Only when we have completed this exercise can we make decisions for the future – plot our future course.

Is there anything in the future that is already becoming visible? To find an answer to this question is much more difficult than looking at the past. For the future still has to come about, of course. And yet, our decisions are influenced by our *sense of the future*, be it consciously or unconsciously. We sometimes speak of premonition. What this is, actually, is that we observe with our will, with that part of us that has not yet passed through our reason, but rises to the surface out of the depths. We probe the future with our will. If we did not do this, if we were only led by what we had learned from the past, we would function like a computer. All we would have to do would be to run the past through our computer, and it would tell us exactly what to decide and what to do. It is a fundamental human trait, however, that our decisions are in part determined by the future, by what is not there yet, by what is still up in the air, so to speak. This already lies concealed in our unconscious will impulses, but has not yet been absorbed in conscious thought. I want to make a few points about this.

One way to approach this area is to examine the things about which we will have to make *decisions* before too long, choices we will have to make. This may be something related to our work, or to our private life. We have an opportunity for early retirement, for instance, and

we are not sure whether we should take advantage of this or not. Or
there is a chance we may get shunted into a dead-end job, which is
actually tempting because work will be much more easy-going; we
may finally have time for all those things we had always wanted to do.
This is the kind of issue that may come up in our work life, and we
have to be quite honest in asking ourselves what it is we really want
to do, and whether our decision fits in our biography.

The same goes for decisions concerning our private life. It may be
that at home things are getting more and more tense. It may look
as if within a year or so we may face decisions about our marriage.
Or, we have lived in the same home for thirty years, but now that
our youngest is about to move into her own apartment, the house
is getting a little too much for us. Should we move? Or a question
of one of my male course participants 'How am I going to manage
my high-pressure job now that my wife also wants to go to work? My
entire world is falling apart.' Or another course participant 'In order
to get ahead, I will have to undertake a heavy study program. How,
for heaven's sake, am I going to manage that without compromising
my family life? Or should I just forget about further promotion?'
These questions about matters you can see coming are often quite to
the point, and sometimes urgent. Even though it has not happened
yet, it is already almost tangible.

Of course we can put off these questions and say 'Have another
drink, and forget about it for now'. And perhaps the problems will
actually disappear – for a while. But inevitably they will return.
Sooner or later we will have to deal with them. What is important is
to give these questions a lot of thought, and not to rush into the most
facile solution just to get rid of the tension. While it is good to recognize questions about the future, and not to push them aside, it may
be desirable to see what happens when we live with them consciously
for a while, and let them mature. This is very important, I think.

It is also important to check whether the easy answers have
perhaps more to do with our past than with the future. Have we
chosen a certain answer because that is how we always used to solve
that sort of question in the past? But perhaps now we have to do
things differently, perhaps those answers will no longer fit in with
our life in the future.

Finally, we may hope that the decision will be made for us. That is
also a possibility. Whether we will be happy with it is another matter.
Yet, this is what many people do.

There is another approach. We may get help from *questions from the world outside*. A third expression from the stage world suggests itself: the audience. We have mentioned the actor, and the stage itself, and now we will take a look at the audience. The audience sometimes has questions for us, too. 'How about this?', 'What about that?' We all know the situation: we have just created some space for ourselves, and have finally achieved some peace and quiet in our life, and then they come and ask 'Would you join our committee?', 'We would like you to take on . . .', etc. – all these kinds of questions that are suddenly dropped in our lap. Then it is important to discover whether these questions are really meant for us, how we should respond to them. We must try to look at this. Does the question fit into our biography? What are we going to do with these questions? Perhaps it is time we stopped doing something we have been doing for a long time. I remember that as a little boy my parents insisted that I take piano lessons. Later on I was dead keen on it myself. I was determined I was going to learn to play the piano, while actually I did not have it in my fingers at all. It was terrible! Three times in my life I started all over again to learn to read music, and to play this music on the piano – to no avail. And there was this piano, standing at home, bought for me specially, and I kept forcing myself. Until I got the feeling, at long last, that I did not have what it takes. The piano was sold. What a relief! And then I discovered I could sing. It went very well. The cramp was gone, and suddenly something new became possible. Everyone knows situations like this. There are stories galore about women who wanted to have a baby in the worst way, but no baby came. After trying everything, a child is adopted, and in no time at all she is pregnant. The cramp is gone, the pressure has disappeared, and as a result there is space for something.

You should keep these images in mind when there are questions coming at you. How cramped up are we when trying to fit an answer into our life? Have we really listened to the signals from the outside? Are these the right questions for us? They can be questions at work, or at home. Or in an association of which we are a member, or in our children's school. Is it really me they need, or are they appealing to me just because I am supposed to be good at it, and have done the same thing so many times elsewhere? Should I take it on, or should I leave it to others for a change, so that they, too, can exercise their talents?

It is important, therefore, that we discriminate between what we should agree to, and what not; that we see where our limits are, and in this way 'organize' our own life. We should keep in mind what abilities we already have, and what we still need to develop. It may be quite a challenge to enter into situations we are not all that confident about, such as executive functions. For we can ourself learn something from it. And perhaps our achievements will be all the more fruitful, not only for ourself, but certainly also for the institution or organization we do the work for, precisely because we have thrown ourself into a challenging task.

This brings me back to my remark that we have to learn to listen to the questions that come to us. It may be quite fruitful that questions come to us that are not all that appealing to us – the kind of questions of which we say 'Why, in heaven's name, do they come to me? I am not qualified for that!' But perhaps others can perceive that we are just the right person. We should take a question like this quite seriously. It may, in fact, fit right into our biography. Time and again I was asked about doing biography work with people. I was running courses, and every time the same question came to me, while I myself was not at all convinced that I should be the one to start doing biography work. Until at a certain point I had to admit 'Apparently they want me, so I'll have to do something about it. I'll have to see to it that I can do something in this direction.' And now that I am doing this work, I can say that not only have the participants in my workshops benefitted, I hope, (this is for them to say, I can't speak for them), but that certainly it has also contributed to my own development.

This was the kind of question, therefore, that can serve as an example of how we have to take seriously all requests that come our way. We should not just give in, particularly not if the question concerns something familiar to us, or something easy, or something that would make us look good without much of an effort – questions regarding matters that come easily to us. But neither should we dismiss out of hand any request because it appears it is not up our alley. For perhaps in the future it *will* be. It is important to be able to say 'No', as long as we know when to say it.

A third approach towards an awakening to what meets us from the future is to concern ourselves with the question of *where we can experience a challenge*. We should not merely ask ourselves what we would *like* to do, but what, really, we *should* do. This can be in relation to the situation at home, but it can also have to do with the other side of the world. What might we do about certain problems in South America, for instance?

It may be of help to make a list of 'things I should be doing'. When this list has been completed, we should take a very critical look at it. We can ask for help from others and 'shake the sieve' to see what gets left over. It is important that we make a distinction between the items that are on that list because they are meaningful, and those that are merely there because they would be fun to do. It is also important to see what is new on the list, and what is part of our past existence. And what among the 'old' items might be rejuvenated. Or what should be omitted from the list altogether. Could we conclude, when we have a good look at our list, that a certain period should be brought to a close? If we evaluate this frankly (and the help of others in this is often quite useful), we should be able to arrive at a meaningful conclusion.

What counts is that we find out to which *ideals* for the future we feel a connection. What challenges us? Where do we feel we should take initiatives? Does our relationship need a new impulse, for instance? Do we have to learn to look at our partner, at the male-female polarity in our relationship, in a different way? Do we have to set aside the old relationship between us to make room for the true ideals we share?

It may also be a case of ideals less close to home. Should we take initiatives with respect to the third world, for instance? We may already feel strongly about third-world issues.

Where is our task? Do we have a connection to certain problems that have the character of a task for us? Bernard Lievegoed calls this 'Working with your surplus forces'. To use, to apply our surplus, that which can be made available. To get involved where we have the feeling 'This has something to do with me, this is of concern to me, this is my connection with the great challenges of our time'.

It may also be that for a long time we have had the feeling that there is a certain unrealized potential in us that we want to develop, like a seed that has not sprouted. It may be a good idea to stop and think about this and ask ourselves whether the time may have come to do something about it, to make the seed sprout.

I also think there is an important biographic secret in consciously *rounding* things *off*. This is especially relevant for older people.

Which are the things in our life that have to be finalized, that have to be given the final touch?

We can make a comparison with photography. When we develop pictures, there comes a point at which they are ready, developed. We can leave them in the developer, but this does not do them any good – the development process has already been completed. This is how it can be with respect to all kinds of matters in life, too. This can be quite painful – for instance if we discover that our relationship is 'overdeveloped'. It is not easy to have to come to the conclusion that for the further development of the partners it is perhaps desirable that they both step into a different 'development bath'. To make space for this, both to the benefit of the other and oneself, is painful. But it can be quite rewarding. For there are always new places where the partners can grow further, although separately instead of together. When we do this rounding off with due care and attention – when the accounts are balanced with sensitivity, and a phase of life is consciously brought to a close, a new future can begin, provided the new initiatives are started with equal care. Then we can say that the old phase of life took its proper course, not that it was wrong. It had its time.

It is also important to perceive why we did certain things we now want to end. I had someone in a course who said about his job 'It did not really suit me, but I owed it to my father to do it. I had to finish it for his sake. It was an inheritance, as it were. But now it is finished. Now I am going to start something new, something of my own.' Because he understood this, this man had not at all the feeling that the old job had been wrong, and the new one right. The new vocation, however, was relevant to what was still coming – it was part of his own future task, while the old occupation was part of his previous task.

To work on our biography means, therefore, that we try to get a feel for our 'inheritance', which we have to manage and bring to completion, terminate, and for the new 'capital' we have to raise. It could also be formulated thus: We have brought something along from before birth, as an inheritance, which we have to round off. But besides, and subsequently, we have to start something new, put something new into motion – something for our own future and that of mankind. This is what I call *old karma* and *new karma*. The old karma is what we brought along – it is the baggage we picked up before birth, which, perhaps, was left over from a previous earth life. (Those who can not relate directly to the idea of reincarnation can still appreciate the imagery, perhaps.) And new karma is created in our life on earth. It is what remains after death, the new forces and impulses we have given to the world and what we have set into motion in our own development. And this new karma, evidently, creates further obligations for the future. The two kinds of karma can overlap, of course.

Old Karma   New Karma

Thus, perhaps, we have gradually gained some insight into the complexity and totality of the eternal human task inscribed on the temple of Apollo at Delphi:

Man, know thyself!

Now that we have gained some understanding of our past and how we relate to it, and of our relation to that which already announces itself from the future, it could be helpful to make up a list of all the things we are – a long list of 'I am . . .' items. The items we are not all that pleased with have to go on it, too. And also all the paradoxes in ourself. It will be a long list, and we have to be as honest with ourself as we can. Are we a knight or a bandit? Or perhaps both? Are we a 'Mary' or an 'Eve'. Or is the ancient idea that Mary and Eve are one and the same also applicable to us? Are we "successful" at work, or do we 'blow it' every so often?

And then we come to the difficult question of whether we want to take responsibility for all these 'selves', all these sub-personalities, as they are called in psychosynthesis. Do we want to be our own 'stage director' (to stay with stage terminology)? Do we also include the negative sides of ourself in our stage production? How do we relate to them? What was our own contribution to their development? And what were the side effects of the development of these more problematic parts of ourself. Does this still have some positive aspect, perhaps, so that in a way we can be thankful for these attributes?

When we have made this long list, as candidly as possible, we must try and place a name tag on the whole thing. What kind of character, what kind of person appears when we look at this list objectively? Help from a concerned, supportive group is also important here. Together with such a group one may discover what kind of human being becomes visible. Are we a fighter? Do we always look for trouble? Or are we mainly a healer, a restorer, someone who puts things back together? Are we an adventurer, a thrill-seeker? In short: What is the essence of what we see on this 'I-am' list?

Before we conclude this looking into our own being and impulses, and enter into our future, we have to come to a *judgement* about it. This is particularly important for those who feel strongly that something has to change in the future. We have made an inventory of our questions, and before we can make decisions for the future, we will have to know how we feel about ourself and our present situation. At an earlier stage there was no point in making judgements. We were concerned with the facts, with collecting data. But now we should ask ourself how we feel about it all. Do we really want to be this knight, or this searcher, or this fighter? What do our feelings tell us about ourself?

What is important here is that we do not judge as the actor, or as the audience. No, we have to sit in the director's chair. We have to raise ourself above it all, but without becoming an outsider. Only then can we become the one who, at the turning point from past to future, can initiate his/her future. We can then take care that the lines originating in the past are not simply extended into the future, and also that the future is not determined by fantasies that have nothing to do with the past at all.

The former way of dealing inwardly with the future can be recognized in expressions such as 'There is nothing new under the sun', or 'Once a thief, always a thief'. This is the world conception of causality, of predictability, and accordingly of denial of freedom, of extrapolation and determinism. The other extreme in a relation to the future is apparent in the concept of the 'blank page', and has the character, therefore, of dissoluteness, of disconnectedness. These are the two polarities, of rigidity on the one side and chaos on the other, or, in biographic terms, a future determined absolutely by the past, as opposed to a future absolutely independent of the past. The *biographic reality* lies in between.

If I am not mistaken, a world conception leaning towards the idea of being chained to the past has in this day and age the upper hand. The ability to deal with the future realistically depends on striking a fruitful, individual balance between two extremes. It is obvious that on the one hand we are bound by a number of given factors – physical attributes, for instance – but on the other hand we can deal creatively with many other given factors, those that are part of our non-physical being such as temperament and character. The freedom of each individual lies in what he/she does with these factors. That is why we see twins take different paths. It is also the reason why one child from a problematic background can straighten him/herself out, while another can not.

In forming our future, therefore, we need to view past, present *and* future from today's perspective.

Chapter Four

Making choices for the future

The time has now come to make an active connection with the future, to choose, to take steps, and to decide. We have to chart our course, and in doing so we have to keep a number of things in mind.

In the first place, we have to realize that *not* to make a decision also has consequences. And the future can never be thought out logically because we can never forsee all of the consequences. The past is something we know. With respect to the present we have a certain feeling. But the future, although it may have announced itself, is still largely shrouded in mist. We can enter the future only with our *will*. The decisions we make with regard to the future are decisions of the will. Because of our impulses of will we can make choices – sometimes aided by our intuition, (which in this context has a dimension different from that of having feelings about events). The choices we make are in between the unrealistic 'everything-is-possible' and the immutable 'everything-is-fixed'.

Our will has nothing to do with fantasy, nor with wishes. It lies much deeper. We only become aware of our will when we act. A wish is just something we think up, something from our head. Of course we may have wishes for our future, but with that we make no future. Our future originates in our will. The objective of a biography study is to become to some extent aware of this unconscious will.

So, we form the future, the still unknown world of tomorrow, with our will. How, then, do we discern this future? One thing that is helpful is to look for the way our will worked in the past. How did the important life decisions we made in the past come about? In order to discover this, we should try to summarize them. What kind of person is indicated by this? What kinds of decisions are these? At the same time we have to ask ourself whether these are also the kinds of decisions that are valid for the future. This is not necessarily the case. We are not stuck forever with one kind of decision-making, for that would mean we function like a computer again.

I once had a man in a biography course with whom I had made this list of important decisions in his life. To his amazement he saw that they were all 'no'-decisions. He could not believe his eyes. When he saw this, he knew right away that this had to be the turning point in his life. And he was then able to give a positive answer to the difficult life question facing him.

We have to 'probe' the future by determining what is already there, what has to take place, and what should not take place. A beautiful image for me is always the one from Wolfram von Eschenbach's *Parzifal*, in which Parzifal rides moodily through the forest until on Good Friday he meets a group of pilgrims, who advise him to go to the hermit Trevrizent. Parzifal overcomes his melancholy and starts looking for Trevrizent, but he is unsuccessful in finding the hermit. At a certain moment he exclaims 'Go as God wills!', lays the reins over his horse's head (the horse is the symbol of the will), and happily spurs his mount into a gallop. The horse then finds the way. The encounter with Trevrizent becomes a turning point in Parzifal's life because Trevrizent teaches him, and as a result removes his sin.

In ancient times people presented their decisions to the gods for judgement, or they went to a sage or soothsayer. Everyone knows the stories about the Oracle of Delphi, and the ancient tales of wise men and initiates. Nowadays it still happens occasionally that parents may fulfill the role of adviser to their children, but as we come closer to selfhood, are more and more self-reliant, more individual, conscious of self, and independent, we have to an increasing degree to make our own choices, with all the pros and cons this entails. Those are the choices that belong to our biography, that fit into the life that is ours, even if it means that we have to face difficult tasks. It is still a leap into the dark, of course, for nothing is as yet truly visible, but choices *must* be made.

And when finally the choice has been made, it is important to look at what has to occur in order for the choice to be carried out. This means working on the *conditions*. For instance, we have decided to enter a new relationship; we now have to work on the conditions for this. What has to occur within ourself and in our environment? Do we have to work on ourself in a certain way – for instance, change something in ourself, get rid of a bad habit, or acquire a new habit? What are the requirements, including quite practical things such as money, time and help. When will our choice become reality? Can we count on any help at all? Will our partner co-operate?

The exciting thing about working on these conditions is that this practical side is already a verification, a test, of our ideals. Do we still want to stick with our choice when we see how much is required, and how much we have to give up? It often turns out that although people want something else, they do not want to give up the pleasant aspects of their old existence. But that may be a consequence of the choice that has been made. How strongly are our choices motivated by our will, and how realistic are they? Perhaps they are far too idealistic, and we will never manage to carry them out. How strongly is our will connected with reality?

What counts in this phase is to discover all this. For an important step in the process we are going through is to test whether what we want to do is true, and really our will.

Chapter Five

Conclusion

We have come to the end of our search, for our self on our life's path, at least for the time being. An attempt has been made below to represent the process in a diagram. It shows a process of *image-forming* with respect to past, present and future. This enables one to arrive at *conclusions* and to make *decisions* with respect to gaining insight into the past, to find a relation to the present, and to make choices for the future. The 'I' is the unifying element, and the vitality of the process is ensured by continuous self-evaluation. Every individual can find in the tasks of life the impulse to go his/her own way.

This is how we can try to make a contribution to the development of humanity through our own 'I', and make part of this development a reality. In this reality our relation to our own biography changes. While at first we might have felt subject to something we call a higher authority (the divine world of ancient times), we gradually gain insight into our own lives and what gives our biography form, and eventually take responsibility for this formation, the formation of our own lives.

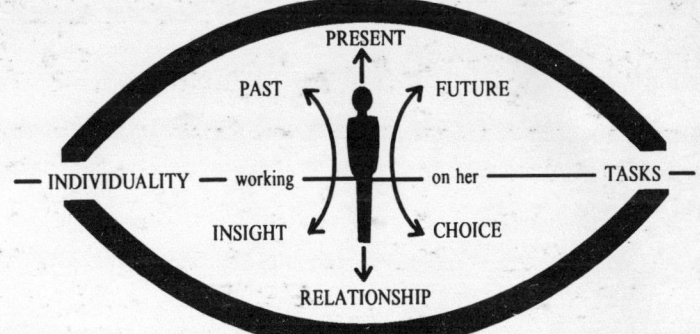

Thus it becomes possible, perhaps, to begin to experience a sense of gratitude for the past because we know now what lessons the past has taught us. But what is at least as important is a sense of trust in our capacity for courage in making decisions for the future. In this way it may eventually become possible to get a glimpse of the individuality, the higher 'I' being, the 'director' who takes responsibility for bringing together everything the actor has to offer, the stage makes possible, and the audience asks for. This is how it may become possible to begin to resemble the one we really are, about whom Schiller, in his *Letters on the Aesthetic Education of Man*, says:

'Each human individual carries within himself a truly ideal human being, according to his talents and his destiny; the great challenge of man's existence is to identify with the immutable unity of this ideal being through all the vicissitudes of life.'

Bibliography

A.H. Bos, *Oordeelsvorming in groepen*, Wageningen 1974

Lex (A.H.) Bos, *Nothing to do with me?* Floris, 1985

Joop van Dam, *Omgaan met het levenslot*, Zeist 1988

Erik H. Erikson, *Identity and the life cycle*, New York/London 1980

Paul Evans & Fernando Bartolomé, *Wordt succes (te) duur betaald?*, Alphen a/d Rijn 1981

Romano Guardini, *Tijdperken des levens*, Tiel/Den Haag 1959

F.H. Julius, *De beeldentaal van de dierenriem*, Zeist 1983

F.H. Julius, *De twaalf driften. De metamorfose van de wil, schets van een kosmisch georiënteerde driften-psychologie*, Zeist 1973

Daniel J. Levinson, *The Season of a Man's Life*, Ballantine, N.Y. 1978

Bernard Lievegoed, *Phases*, Rudolf Steiner Press, London 1975

Bernard Lievegoed, *Lezingen en essays 1953-1986*, Zeist 1987

Bernard Lievegoed, *Man on the Threshold*, Hawthorn Press 1984

Leo G.M. Prick, *Demonen van de middag*, Baarn 1984

H.C. Rümke, *Levenstijdperken van de man*, Amsterdam 1973

Signe Schäfer, Betty Staley & Margli Matthews, *Ariadne's Awakening*, Hawthorn Press, Stroud, U.K. 1984

Friedrich Schiller, *The Aesthetic Education of Man*, 1984

Jerry Schöttelndreier, 'Biografie-studie, een opgave', in *Tijdschrift voor sociale hulpverlening vanuit de antroposofie*, December 1987, themanummer 'Biografie en hulpverlening', Driebergen 1987

Rudolf Steiner, The Four Temperaments, Anthroposophic Press, NY 1971

Max Stibbe, *Mensetypen*, Rotterdam 1978

W.F. Veltman, *Karma en rëincarnatie*, Zeist 1981

Penelope Washbourn, *Fasen in het leven van de vrouw*, Rotterdam 1985

A.J. Welman, *De menselijke levensloop. Een psychotherapeutische benadering met behulp van sprookjesbeelden*, Zeist 1987

Wolfram von Eschenbach, *Parzival*, Vintage Books, N.Y. 1961

Marguerite Yourcenar, *Het hermetisch zwart* (L'oeuvre au noir), Vertaald door Jenny Tuin, Amsterdam 1988, p. 127 (op. cit p.6)

Biography and Self Development Series.

Various books are planned on biography work and self development. The need for these has arisen from 'biography work' – which involves taking stock, considering the events, patterns, themes, questions forming one's biography or 'writing in life'. This can be done in a group setting, for example a biography workshop, or in one-to-one biographical counselling. Biography exercises are used in management development, personal effectiveness workshops, career planning, men's groups, women's groups, to mention a few applications.

So far, the most widely known Hawthorn publication in this field is *Springboard – a Women's Development workbook* which won the 1989 Lady Platt award for innovative equal opportunities training for the BBC.

Liz Willis and Jenny Daisley included a chapter on *Biography* work.

Other relevant publications include *Man on the Threshold*, *The Twelve Senses*, *Soulways*, *Ariadne's Awakening*, and *How to transform thinking, feeling and willing*.

Martin Large.
Hawthorn Press 1991.

THE TWELVE SENSES
Albert Soesman.
Translated by Jakob Cornelis

The senses both nourish our experience as 'well springs' and act as windows on the world. But overstimulation may undermine healthy sense experiences. *The Twelve Senses* gives a lively way of both experiencing and understanding the human senses.

Albert Soesman explores not merely the normal five senses, but twelve senses. These are the senses of touch, life, self-movement, balance, smell, taste, vision, temperature, hearing, language, the conceptual and the ego senses. The development, expression and functioning of each sense is described. The senses are discussed in physical, soul and spiritual/social groups, contrasted as polarities, distinguished as 'inner' or 'outer', and each sense related to the signs of the zodiac.

The author's imaginative approach to the senses will be useful as an accessible study guide for teachers, doctors, therapists, counsellors, psychologists and scientists.

210x135mm; 178pp; Social Ecology Series;
ISBN I 869 890 22 I.

MAN ON THE THRESHOLD
Bernard Lievegoed.

Humanity is crossing a major threshold. The boundaries that surrounded consciousness centuries ago are no longer fixed, and it is not only the physical world which implies reality. Instead of voyages of discovery to unknown continents, the exploration of inner frontiers is taking place. This may be overpowering, as in the case of psychological disturbances and mental illness, or it may be enlightening and positive.

The theme of *Man on the Threshold* is inner development. Seeds for growth hidden within each individuality are described along with maps and guidelines for those either undertaking an inner journey, or wishing to work therapeutically with others who are.

Ancient and alternative paths are described – Egyptian and Northern init iation mysteries, the Christian Rosicrucian path, the Eastern ways and the medieval Christian approach. This leads to a practical outlineof an anthroposophical approach to inner training and development. The manifold aspects of the human double are examined. Physiological and psychological factors in our relationship to earth, sun, moon and planets are described at length along with medical and social implications.

Professor Lievegoed is a distinguished physician, educator, and industrial psychologist. The *Golden Quill* literary award of the Netherlands Publishers' Association was given to Professor Lievegoed on the publication of *Man on the Threshold* in December 1983. This award honours those making a significant contribution to Dutch cultural life. He was described as 'a true contemporary, a man who takes note of the issues of his time and of the needs of a turbulent world.'

The merit (of Lievegoed's books) is, above all, their evocatory effect. They urge one, impel one to go to work, to put into practice what one has read – either in one's own personal life, or in social life. . .

210x135mm; paperback; 224pp; Social Ecology Series
ISBN 0 950 7062 64

SOULWAYS
The developing soul-life phases, thresholds and biography.
Rudolf Treichler.
Translated by Anna Meuss.

Soulways offers insights into personal growth through the phases and turning points of human life. A profound picture of both child and adult development is given. The developmental needs, potentials and questions of each life phase and passage are mapped. This challenges readers to reflecton their own biographies.
    Drawing on his work as a psychiatrist, Dr Rudolf Treichler explores the developmental disorders of soul life: e.g. addictions, inner emptiness, neurosis, premature ageing, psychosis, mid life questions, hysteria, epilepsy, anorexia, schizophrenia, depression and mania.
    Such disorders are explored from a developmental and therapeutic viewpoint – as questions which may challenge individual growth.
    Soulways will be a useful guide for counsellors, parents, teachers, doctors, therapists, and those doing biography work.

210x135mm; 320pp; Social Ecology Series;
ISBN I 869 890 13 2.

ARIADNE'S AWAKENING
Taking up the threads of consciousness
Signe Schaefer, Betty Staley and Margli Matthews

Much has been written about women and men in terms of roles, gender and social forms through the ages. The past two decades have witnessed widespread change in 'rights' and 'equality' on external levels, but this has not always made for more human fulfilment. The authors acknowledge the context of feminism, but broaden its picture enormously. They view 'masculine' and 'feminine' not just as bodily forms, but as principles of meaning: principles at work within each of us, in society and indeed in the entire span of evolution.

Ariadne's Awakening traces through myth and history the journey humankind has made up to the present; it considers phases of life, relationships for men and women, and confronts such issues as the scientific management of conception and death, the rape of Earth's natural resources and the need for a New Feminine to influence values and decisions for the future.

Signe Schaefer, Betty Staley and Margli Matthews have raised families while also teaching and researching current social questions. This book is the outcome of over a decade's work with women's groups in Britain, Holland and America.

210x135mm; 212pp;
ISBN 1 869 890 01 9

HOW TO TRANSFORM THINKING FEELING AND WILLING
Practical exercises for the training of thinking, feeling, willing, imagination, composure, intuition, positivity and wonder.
Jörgen Smit
Translated by Simon Blaxland de Lange.

A path of transforming thinking, feeling and willing is described in this book. Practical exercises for the illuminating and strengthening of thinking are given. There are exercises for the development of a living inner imagination, for concentration, for vivid feeling and for contemplating the day's events so as to deepen one's thinking capacities. The development of inspiration and intuition is explored, as well as the qualities of composure, reverence, open-mindedness and wonder.

Jörgen Smit aims to enable readers to follow a meditative path leading to deepening insight and awareness.

The author works with young people from the Goetheanum, the centre of the Anthroposophical Society founded by Rudolf Steiner (1861–1925) near Basle, Switzerland. He was born in 1916 in Bergen, Norway and he worked as a Waldorf teacher for thirty years, and in teacher training.

210x135mm; 64pp;
ISBN I 869 890 17 5.

SPRINGBOARD
Liz Willis and Jenny Daisley.

Springboard is a practical self development workbook aiming to enable women of all ages to take the next steps in their development more effectively.

This book is the first of its kind in the U.K. and has been specifically written for non-management women to work through for themselves, and for use by in-company training specialists wanting to initiate effective women's development on a large scale.

The 250 pages are full of exercises, examples, tips and ideas, written in a down to earth style and with a wholistic approach and illustrated with cartoons by Viv Quillan.

Liz Willis and Jenny Daisley are two of the U.K.'s leading women's development specialists. Liz Willis set up the Pepperell Unit for Women's Development at the Industrial Society and currently works as an independent development consultant. Jenny Daisley specialises in developing new forms of training and learning: for example biography work and wholistic development.

Springboard won the Lady Platt Award 1989 for innovative equal opportunities training. It has had good reviews in the *Times*, the *Guardian*, *She*, *Cosmopolitan*, *Woman's Journal* and was *Good Housekeeping's* reader's October treat of the month.

"A month after finishing the book I was promoted. Coincidence? I don't think so! I'm now in a position that I've long thought I would be good at, but had previously not had the self confidence to apply for."
Jennifer Davies, Assistant Senior Studio Manager, BBC World Services

"This workbook will be invaluable for women who are re-discovering their potential. It is full of practical advice, but most importantly, it is a real confidence booster."
Brenda Dean, General Secretary, SOGAT

*"**Springboard** leads to career take-off . . . brilliantly simple idea . . . a unique development training programme for women."*
Wendy Jack, Glasgow Herald

"It will help many women at a variety of stages. It's well planned, easy to follow, and offers a great boost to self esteem through self help. It's full of good advice and sound good sence."
Anna Ford, BBC Television News

"Inspir-actical" is how I'd describe **Springboard.** *It inspires women to decide what they most want to achieve and then, very practically, helps them to do it. It's fun and involving."*
Valerie Hammond, Director, Ashridge Management Research Group

A4 Size: 29 × 21cm; 288pp, sewn paperback ISBN I 869 890 191.

Books on Biography and Self Development

Ariadne's Awakening
How to Transform Thinking, Feeling and Willing
Man on the Threshold
Springboard
The Twelve Senses

If you have difficulties ordering from a bookshop, you can order direct from Hawthorn Press, Bankfield House, 13 Wallbridge, Stroud, Glos. GL5 3JA, U.K. Telephone (0453) 757040.
Fax (0453) 753295.